Rose Hair Tarantula
Pet Tarantula
Chilean Rose Tarantula

Publish by Gohas 2016

Copyright and Trademarks. This publication is Copyright 2016 by Gohas. All products, publications and services mentioned and recommended in this publication are protected by trademarks. In such instance, all trademarks & copyright belong to the respective owners.

All rights reserved. No part of this book may be reproduced or transferred in any form or by any means, graphic, electronic, or mechanical, including photocopying, recording, taping, or by any information storage retrieval system, without the written permission of the author. Pictures used in this book are either royalty free pictures bought from stock-photo websites or have the source mentioned underneath the picture.

Disclaimer and Legal Notice. This product is not legal or medical advice and should not be interpreted in that manner. You need to do your own due-diligence to determine if the content of this right for you. The author and affiliates of this product are not liable for any damages or losses associated with the content in this book. While every attempt has been made to verify the information shared in this publication, neither the author nor the affiliates assume any responsibility for errors, omissions or contrary interpretation of the subject matter herein. Any perceived slights to any specific person(s) or organization(s) are purely unintentional.

We have no control over the nature, content and availability of the websites listed in this book. The inclusion of any websites links does not necessarily imply a recommendation or endorse the views expressed within them. Gohas takes no responsibility for, and will not be liable for, the websites being temporarily unavailable or being removed from the internet. The accuracy and completeness of information provided herein and opinions stated herein are not guaranteed or warranted to produce any particular results, and the advice and strategies, contained herein may not be suitable for every individual. The author shall not be liable for any loss incurred as a consequence of the use and application, directly or indirectly, of any information in regards to the subject matter covered.

The prices quoted in this book to be paid for Tarantulas are not exact, they are a guide only, and should be treated as such.

Rose Hair Tarantula

The Complete Owner's Guide

Including Information on Care, Cage Setup, Feeding, Handling, Breeding and More.

Foreword

The rose hair tarantula is a unique and beautiful arachnid that makes a great pet. These tarantulas have lovely rose-colored hair and they are generally a docile species. If you have ever thought about keeping a tarantula as a pet, the rose hair tarantula is a great option. Within the pages of this book you will find a wealth of information about this beautiful species including enough information to help you decide whether or not it is the right pet for you. If it is, the information in this book will have you well on your way to becoming the best pet owner you can be.

Table of Contents

Introduction 10
   Useful Terms to Know 12
Chapter One: Understanding Rose Hair Tarantulas 16
   1.) What Are Rose Hair Tarantulas? 17
   2.) Facts About Rose Hair Tarantulas 19
      Summary of Rose Hair Tarantula Facts 22
   3. History of Rose Hair Tarantulas 24
   4.) Types of Tarantulas 26
Chapter Two: What to Know Before You Buy Your Tarantula 37
   1.) Do You Need a License? 38
   2.) How Many Should You Buy? 40
   3.) Can Tarantulas Be Kept with Other Pets? 42
   4.) Cost of Caring for Tarantulas 43
      Initial Costs 43
      Monthly Costs 46
   5.) Pros and Cons for Rose Hair Tarantulas 49
Chapter Three: Purchasing Rose Hair Tarantulas 51
   1.) Where to Buy Rose Hair Tarantulas 52
   2.) Selecting a Supplier or Breeder 53
   3.) Picking a Healthy Tarantula 55

Chapter Four: Preparing Your Tarantula Cage...............57
    1.) Basic Habitat Requirements......................................58
    2.) Setting Up the Cage 61
    3.) Lighting and Heating Requirements.......................64
    4.) Cage Cleaning and Maintenance 66

Chapter Five: Feeding Your Tarantula................................68
    1.) Basic Nutritional Needs 69
    2.) Types of Tarantula Food 71
    3.) Feeding Tips for Tarantulas......................................72

Chapter Six: Breeding Rose Hair Tarantulas....................73
    1.) Basic Breeding Information 74
    2.) Tips for Breeding Your Tarantula............................76

Chapter Seven: Keeping Your Tarantula Healthy...........79
    1.) Common Health Problems 80
    Bad Molt...81
    Dehydration 82
    Fungal Infection 83
    Mites 84
    Nematode Worms 85
    Trauma 86
    2.) Tips for Preventing Disease......................................87

Chapter Eight: Frequently Asked Questions....................89

Chapter Nine: Rose Hair Tarantula Care Sheet 94

    1.) Basic Information 95

    2.) Habitat Set-Up Information 97

    3.) Feeding Information 98

    4.) Breeding Information 99

Chapter Ten: Relevant Websites 101

    1.) Cages for Rose Hair Tarantulas 102

    2.) Cage Accessories and Decorations 104

    3.) Food for Rose Hair Tarantulas 106

    4.) Additional Resources and Supplies 108

Index 110

Photo Credits 118

References 123

Introduction

When you hear the word "tarantula," what comes to mind? Do you picture a large, hairy spider with a lethal bite? Or perhaps a monster that comes crawling out of your nightmares? Many people are familiar with tarantulas only on the most basic level – they do not realize that most tarantulas are actually very docile and they generally do not bite unless they feel threatened. One such tarantula species is the Chilean rose hair tarantula – or simply the rose hair tarantula.

The rose hair tarantula is a fairly large arachnid, having a leg span up to six inches wide. What makes these tarantulas

Introduction

unique is the patch of rose-colored hair on their backs. Rose hair tarantulas are one of the most common species of pet tarantula and they can make excellent pets, even for inexperienced owners. These tarantulas are generally very easy to care for and they can live for many years.

If you have ever thought about keeping a tarantula as a pet, the rose hair tarantula is an excellent species to start with. Before you go out and buy one, however, you should educate yourself about the species and learn everything you can about what it takes to keep a rose hair tarantula happy and healthy. That is where this book comes in. In this book you will find a wealth of information not only about the rose hair tarantula species, but you will also receive specific information and step-by-step guides for preparing a habitat for your tarantula and for delivering the highest quality of care possible. By the time you finish this book you will have a firm understanding of the rose hair tarantula and you will be able to make an educated decision regarding whether or not this is the right pet for you.

Introduction

Useful Terms to Know

Abdomen – the hindmost part of the tarantula's body, also known as the opithosoma; contains most of the vital organs

Anterior – closer to the front end

Arachnid – a species belonging to the class Arachnida; this includes spiders, mites, ticks, and scorpions

Arachnologist – a person who studies arachnids

Autotomy – also known as autospasy; the act of voluntarily dropping a limb in response to danger or to free itself

Carapace – the hard shield-like covering that protects the spider's body

Cardiac Mark – a mark on the midline of the abdomen over the heart; also known as the heart mark

Cephalothorax – the forward-most section of the spider's body; also known as the prosoma

Chelicera – mouthparts that are tipped with fangs; jaws

Introduction

Cheliceral Furrow – a groove at the end of the jaw where the fangs fit snugly; the fangs fold out from this furrow

Coxa – the first segment of each leg that is attached to the cephalothorax

Cuticle – the chitinous protein that makes up the exoskeleton and other body parts

Diurnal – refers to an animal that is active during the day

Dorsal – the upper surface

Epigynum – the part of a female spider that covers the internal genitalia, located on the underside of the abdomen

Exoskeleton – the hard shell covering the outside of the body for arthropods

Exuvia – the shed exoskeleton left after a spider molts

Hemolymph – a fluid found in some invertebrates which acts like blood, carrying oxygen throughout the body

Invertebrate – an animal lacking a backbone; invert

Lateral – having to do with the side

Introduction

Metatarsus – the sixth segment of each leg

Molt – a process through which spiders shed their old exoskeleton as a new one grows in

Mygalomorph – a primitive version of the spider that is heavy in body and stout legged; tarantulas are included

Nocturnal – referring to an animal that is active at night

Pedicel – the narrow portion of the body connecting the abdomen and the cephalothorax

Pedipalps – the leg-like appendages surrounding the jaws used to manipulate food

Posterior – closer to the back end

Seta – hair

Sexual Dimorphism – refers to physical differences between males and females of the same species

Silk – a kind of liquid protein secreted from the spider's spinning glands

Spiderling – a baby spider

Spinnerets – the finger-like silk spinning organs

Tarsus – the final (7th) segment of the leg

Introduction

Trichobothrium – the long sensory hairs that grow from the leg; used to sense vibrations and wind currents

Urticating Hairs – the barb-covered hairs found on the abdomen in most tarantulas

Ventral – having to do with the underside

Venom – a substance that is designed to paralyze a spider's prey; may also be used as a defense mechanism

Chapter One: Understanding Rose Hair Tarantulas

The rose hair tarantula is a very interesting creature for a number of reasons. Not only is it a giant spider, but it has a unique appearance and a gentle demeanor – not what you would expect from a large arachnid. If you are thinking about keeping a rose tarantula as a pet, take the time to learn everything you can about these wonderful creatures. In this chapter you will find a wealth of information about the rose hair tarantula in general including rose hair tarantula facts, history and information about other types of pet tarantulas.

Chapter One: Understanding Rose Hair Tarantulas

1.) What Are Rose Hair Tarantulas?

The rose hair tarantula is possibly the most common species of tarantula kept as a pet in both the United States and Europe. This species is known by several names including the Chilean rose tarantula, the Chilean red-haired tarantula, and the Chilean fire tarantula. A tarantula is a type of large, hairy arachnid that belongs to the Theraphosidae family of spiders which consists of about 900 different species (there may be many more that have yet to be identified).

For the most part, tarantulas are not dangerous to humans and several species – like the rose hair tarantula – have become common in the exotic pet trade. The tarantula is a type of arthropod which means that it is an invertebrate that has an exoskeleton rather than an endoskeleton. The tarantula's body is comprised of two parts – the cephalothorax (or prosoma) and the abdomen (or opisthosoma). These two parts are connected by a narrow section called the pedicel and it is flexible enough to allow both parts a wide range of motion.

Tarantulas vary greatly in size from one species to another with some species growing up to the size of a dinner plate while others remain as small as a fingernail. The actual body length of most tarantulas is between 1 and

Chapter One: Understanding Rose Hair Tarantulas

4 inches (2.5 to 10cm), though leg spans can vary greatly from about 3 to 12 inches (8 to 30cm). The leg span of a tarantula is measured from the tip of the back leg on one side to the tip of the front leg on the opposite side.

Chapter One: Understanding Rose Hair Tarantulas

2.) Facts About Rose Hair Tarantulas

The rose hair tarantula is a species belonging to the Theraphosidae family and it is the most common species sold in the pet trade in the United States and Europe. This species is native to Chile, though it can be found in desert and scrub regions of Bolivia and Argentina as well. The rose hair tarantula is named for the color of the hairs covering its body. These spiders have dark brown or black bodies covered with a coating of reddish or rose-colored hairs. Males of the species are often more colorful than females and they have a fuzzier appearance.

Chapter One: Understanding Rose Hair Tarantulas

Rose hair tarantulas are a fairly large species, reaching maturity between 3 and 4 years with a leg span around 5 inches (12.5cm). This species is generally very docile which is what makes it so popular in the pet trade – it is also a fairly low-maintenance species. The rose hair tarantula can be somewhat skittish, preferring to run away from danger rather than becoming defensive, but it does have the ability to bite if it needs to defend itself. This species also has urticating hairs on the abdomen which can be ejected as a defense mechanism – these hairs can be very irritating when they become embedded in the skin or eyes.

In the wild, the rose hair tarantula is a nocturnal species that feeds primarily on insects. In captivity, this tarantula will feed on a variety of insects including crickets, locusts, grasshoppers, cockroaches, mealworms, and more. When it comes to keeping this species in captivity, it should be kept in a terrarium with regulated temperature and humidity levels. This is easy to accomplish, however, with the use of a heat mat and a lighting system. Rose hair tarantulas are generally easy to care for in captivity.

When it comes to breeding the rose hair tarantula, this species reproduces fairly easily in captivity and it has been bred for research for many years. Females of the species may benefit from a cooling period of several months to prepare them for breeding and, if the mating is successful,

Chapter One: Understanding Rose Hair Tarantulas

the female will produce an egg sac containing around 500 eggs. Males of the species typically die within a few weeks of mating which is why their average lifespan is so much shorter than that of the female rose hair tarantula.

In general, rose hair tarantulas are a hardy species that tends to fare well in captivity. These tarantulas do go through a molting period during which they shed their exoskeleton in order to grow. Young tarantulas might molt several times per year while they are still growing but a full-grown tarantula will only molt once every year or so. You can predict when a tarantula is about to molt because its exoskeleton will darken and the tarantula will likely become lethargic and may stop eating. When the molt actually starts, the tarantula might lie on its back and become inactive – it is important not to disturb the spider during molting and it can take the tarantula as little as a few days or as long as several weeks to recover from a molt.

Chapter One: Understanding Rose Hair Tarantulas

Summary of Rose Hair Tarantula Facts

Scientific Name: *Grammastola rosea*

Taxonomy: family Theraphosidae

Country of Origin: Chile

Distribution: northern Chile, Argentina, and Bolivia

Habitat: desert and scrub regions

Size: average 5-inch (12.5cm) leg span

Maturity: reach adult size between 3 and 4 years

Color: dark brown to black with a coat of reddish or pink hairs on the body

Anatomy: two-part body covered in an exoskeleton; eight legs, each with seven segments

Molting: shedding the exoskeleton in order to grow; young tarantulas might molt several times a year, mature tarantulas once a year or less

Temperament: docile and low-maintenance

Lifespan (~~male~~ female): average 15 to 20 years

Lifespan (~~female~~ male): average 4 to 5 years

Chapter One: Understanding Rose Hair Tarantulas

Diet: primarily insects including crickets, locusts, grasshoppers, cockroaches, mealworms, etc.

Breeding: breed fairly easily in captivity; females produce egg sacs containing about 500 eggs

Sexual Dimorphism: males have longer legs and a fuzzier appearance; females are stocky and bulky

Chapter One: Understanding Rose Hair Tarantulas

3. History of Rose Hair Tarantulas

The first spider to carry the name "tarantula" was a species of wolf spider known by the scientific name *Lycosa tarantula*. The name of this species was derived from the name of an Italian town, Taranto. After this species was identified, the name "tarantula" was given to most of the large, ground-dwelling spiders that were discovered after that point. In reality, the wolf spider is neither as large nor as hairy as most tarantulas, so the usage of the "tarantula" name shifted to refer to members of the Theraphosidae family which contains most modern tarantula species.

The rose hair tarantula was originally described by Walckenaer in the year 1837. The species was given the scientific name *Grammastola rosea* in referred to the rose-colored hairs on the spider's back. This species was originally thought to be a burrowing species, but further observation indicated that the species was simply nocturnal, spending most of the day in a sheltered above-ground web and coming out to hunt at night.

The rose hair tarantula is a very unique species because it comes in several different color morphs – this makes it difficult to determine the correct scientific name for the species. Researchers are still debating whether or not the different color forms are actually different species or simply

Chapter One: Understanding Rose Hair Tarantulas

different morphs. Some scientists believe that there are actual anatomical differences between the color morphs which means that they should be considered separate species. The three color morphs of the rose hair tarantula known to exist are:

- *Grammastola rosea* – the standard of the species
- *Grammastola cala* – the reddish color morph
- *Grammastola spatulata* – the brownish color morph

There is also some confusion between the rose hair tarantula and a related species, *Grammastola porteri*. This species is also endemic to Chile and was first described in 1926. The *Grammastola porter*, known as the Chilean tarantula, is frequently confused with the rose hair tarantula and is often sold as such in pet stores.

Chapter One: Understanding Rose Hair Tarantulas

4.) Types of Tarantulas

Although the rose hair tarantula is by far one of the most popular species of tarantula kept as pets, it is not the only option. Below you will find an overview of some of the other popular species of pet tarantula:

- Mexican Redknee (*Brachypelma smithi*)
- Costa Rican Zebra (*Aphonoplema seemani*)
- Desert Blonde (*Aphonopelma chalcodes*)
- Curly Hair Tarantula (*Brachypelma albopilosum*)
- Mexican Fireleg (*Brachypelma boehmi*)

You will find an overview of each of these popular tarantula species in the coming pages so you can compare them to the rose hair tarantula.

Chapter One: Understanding Rose Hair Tarantulas

Mexican Redknee (*Brachypelma smithi*)

The Mexican Redknee tarantula is a terrestrial species which means that it lives on the ground. This species is native to Mexico where it can be found in the Sierra Madre del Sur and Sierra Madre Occidental mountain ranges. The Mexican Redknee tarantula is a very large species, having a body measuring about 4 inches long with a 6-inch leg span. This species typically weighs about 15 grams at maturity, though the male usually has a smaller mass.

Mexican Redknee tarantulas are a very popular species among tarantula enthusiasts and the females have very long lifespans. Females can live up to 30 years, though males

Chapter One: Understanding Rose Hair Tarantulas

typically only live for about 5 years. Like most tarantulas, the Mexican Redknee has urticating hairs on its abdomen which it can eject if threatened, but this species generally does not bite. This tarantula is considered a very docile species and they are only slightly venomous to humans, though a bite could cause an allergic reaction in some individuals.

This species can be found in deciduous tropical forests throughout southwestern Mexico and it was once listed as an endangered species by CITES due to habitat loss. Exportation is another major threat to this species as is the use of pesticides.

Chapter One: Understanding Rose Hair Tarantulas

Costa Rican Zebra (*Aphonoplema seemani*)

The Costa Rican Zebra tarantula is also sometimes referred to as the striped-knee tarantula due to its coloration. These spiders are typically black with white stripes at the joints of each leg. This species is native to western Costa Rica, though it can also be found in other parts of Central America such as Guatemala, Nicaragua, and Honduras.

Costa Rican Zebra tarantulas are a type of deep-burrowing tarantula and they tend to inhabit open scrublands. This species tends to hide deep in its burrow during the heat of the day then comes out in the evening

Chapter One: Understanding Rose Hair Tarantulas

before it gets too cold to hunt. This species has a leg span up to 13 cm and its diet consists primarily of insects like crickets, grasshoppers, and roaches. The female of the species can live for 20 years or more, though the male usually only lives for about 5 years.

The Costa Rican Zebra tarantula is a very skittish species, so handling is generally not recommended. For this reason it is also not recommended as a beginner species. These tarantulas require higher humidity levels than the rose hair tarantula and they need deeper substrate due to their deep-burrowing habits. This species is not aggressive, but it is very fast and a talented escape artist.

Chapter One: Understanding Rose Hair Tarantulas

Desert Blonde (*Aphonopelma chalcodes*)

Known as the western desert tarantula as well as the desert blonde, this species can be found in limited areas of Arizona and various parts of Mexico. This tarantula is named for the pale hairs covering its body which appear in stark contrast to its dark legs and abdomen. The desert blonde tarantula is a large-bodied spider, growing 3 to 5 inches in length, and they dig large burrows measuring up to 2 inches in diameter.

The desert blonde tarantula lives in the desert, so it is use to harsh weather conditions. This species doesn't need much water to survive and they are largely nocturnal. Both

Chapter One: Understanding Rose Hair Tarantulas

sexes take about 8 to 10 years to mature but females can live for up to 25 years while males usually only last a few months after breeding. This species eats all kinds of insects as well as small lizards and they generally do not pose a threat to humans.

Chapter One: Understanding Rose Hair Tarantulas

Curly Hair Tarantula (*Brachypelma albopilosum*)

Also known as the Honduran curlyhair tarantula, the curly hair tarantula is native to Central American and can be found in parts of Costa Rica as well as Honduras. This species is terrestrial and an opportunistic burrower – this means that it may take over burrows abandoned by rodents and other animals. The curly hair tarantula is named for the long hairs covering its body which have a unique curled appearance.

Curly hair tarantulas have very plump bodies and they are generally dark brown to black in coloration. Their curly

Chapter One: Understanding Rose Hair Tarantulas

hairs have a bronze or gold sheen and the hairs are particularly dense on the hind legs. Males of the species often have a lighter bronze coloration than females and they generally only live about 5 years to the female's 15-year lifespan.

The curly hair tarantula is a popular species kept as a pet and it breeds readily in captivity. These tarantulas are very adaptable to changes in humidity and temperature, though they do prefer warmer temperatures and higher humidity. The curly hair tarantula is a burrowing species so it requires more floor space than height in its cage. This species has a similar diet to the rose hair tarantula, feeding primarily on insects and occasionally small mice.

Mexican Fireleg (*Brachypelma boehmi*)

The Mexican Fireleg tarantula is very similar in appearance to the Mexican Redknee tarantula, having a dramatic orange and black coloration. This species grows up to 6 inches in size, though it grows more slowly than most South American tarantulas. The Mexican Fireleg tarantula is native to Mexico where it can be found in areas along the central Pacific Coast, living in dry scrublands in either self-made or abandoned burrows.

This species of tarantula is very docile. This, combined with its beautiful coloration, makes it a very popular

Chapter One: Understanding Rose Hair Tarantulas

species for a pet. The Mexican Fireleg tarantula is unfortunately threatened by the illegal pet trade as well as habitat destruction – it also doesn't help that it has a high mortality rate before reaching sexual maturity. This species reaches sexual maturity around 7 to 8 years for males and 9 to 10 years for females. Males usually only live up to 1 year after reproduction.

Chapter Two: What to Know Before You Buy Your Tarantula

Having learned a little more about the rose hair tarantula, you should now have a basic idea whether or not this species is the right pet for you. Before you actually make your decision, however, you should take the time to learn about the practical aspects of tarantula care. In this chapter you will learn about licensing requirements for the pet tarantula as well as information about the cost associated with these animals. You will also receive an overview of the pros and cons for keeping rose hair tarantulas as pets.

Chapter Two: What to Know Before You Buy

1.) *Do You Need a License?*

Before you go out and buy a rose hair tarantula, you should first take the time to make sure it is legal to own one in your area. Keep in mind that the tarantula is considered an exotic pet, so the rules may be different than they are for cats and dogs. Different countries and regions have different requirements for keeping and breeding exotic pets, so you might want to check with your local council to see if there are any restrictions in your area. Keep in mind that restrictions might be different for owning a tarantula than they are for breeding or importing them.

In the United States you do not need a license to keep rose hair tarantulas as pets because they are not an endangered species, nor are they considered a dangerous species. You will need a license, however, if you plan to import or export these animals – you can apply for a license on the U.S. Department of Interior Fish and Wildlife Service (USFW) website. You may also need to obtain a license if you plan to breed these tarantulas.

In the United Kingdom, there are no requirements for tarantula owners to obtain a license. There are, however, strict rules regarding the import and export of live animals. You also need to be careful about where you obtain your tarantula – it is illegal to sell or purchase wild-caught

Chapter Two: What to Know Before You Buy

specimens in many areas so only buy a rose hair tarantula from a licensed breeder.

Chapter Two: What to Know Before You Buy

2.) How Many Should You Buy?

When it comes to keeping rose hair tarantulas as a pet, one of the questions you must ask yourself is how many tarantulas you want to keep. If you speak to experienced tarantula owners you will probably receive different answers to this question. Many tarantula keepers advocate for keeping tarantulas alone, though some have had success keeping tarantulas of different species together.

There is no hard-fast evidence to support the idea that two rose hair tarantulas cannot be kept together, though there is little evidence to show that they can either (with the

Chapter Two: What to Know Before You Buy

exception being a male and female of the same species). In the end, it is up to you whether you want to take the risk or not. If you do choose to keep more than one tarantula, be sure you have a terrarium large enough and provide plenty of hiding places just in case.

Chapter Two: What to Know Before You Buy

3.) Can Tarantulas Be Kept with Other Pets?

Keeping a tarantula with another kind of pet is just asking for trouble. Rose hair tarantulas are an insectivorous species, but they may view smaller invertebrates and even small reptiles or amphibians as prey. Keeping a tarantula with a larger animal is also a bad idea because the tarantula may feel threatened. If you plan to keep rose hair tarantulas, your best bet is to keep them singly in individual cages or terrariums.

Chapter Two: What to Know Before You Buy

4.) Cost of Caring for Tarantulas

Before you rush out and buy a pet tarantula, you need to make sure that you can cover the costs associated with tarantula care. Not only do you need to think about how much it costs to buy a tarantula, but you must also purchase and furnish a tank for your new pet. In this section you will learn the basics about what it costs to keep a rose hair tarantula as a pet.

Initial Costs

The initial costs associated with tarantula ownership include the cost to purchase your new pet as well as costs to purchase and furnish your tarantula cage. The initial costs for rose hair tarantulas are summarized below:

Purchase Price – The purchase price for a tarantula will vary depending where you buy it. If you purchase your rose hair tarantula from a pet store your costs might be higher than if you purchase from a breeder or go to a local pet expo. You can expect to spend anywhere from $15 to $40 (£13.50 to £36) for your tarantula.

Chapter Two: What to Know Before You Buy

Tank – The cost to purchase a tank for your tarantula should not be very high because you only need a 5 or 10 gallon tank. You should expect to spend about $10 to $20 (£9 to £18) on your tarantula tank.

Substrate – The amount of substrate you need will depend on the size of your tarantula tank. For the most part, however, you can expect to spend about $10 (£9) on a large bag of substrate that will be enough to get you started.

Decorations – The cost for tank decorations will depend on how lavish you want to be. Tarantulas do not require any fancy decorations – a few rocks, sticks, and pieces of driftwood along with a plant or two will be sufficient. You should aim to spend about $25 to $50 (£22.50 to £45) on tank decorations for your rose hair tarantula.

Lighting and Heating – Rose hair tarantulas do not like intense lighting so you will probably be able to get away with ambient room light. You will, however, need to buy a heating mat to keep your tank warm. A heat mat large enough for a 10-gallon tank will cost you about $15 (£13.50).

Chapter Two: What to Know Before You Buy

If you need to use a heat lamp, your costs may be another $20 (£18) or so higher.

Accessories – In addition to the cost for your tarantula, tank, and tank essentials you will also need to purchase a water bowl, a water bottle for misting the tank, and a tank thermometer and humidity gauge. You may also want to purchase some additional things like rubber gloves for cleaning the tank and a weight to keep the lid weighed down. These costs will vary, but you should budget for about $25 to $50 (£22.50 to £45) be safe.

Initial Costs for Rose Hair Tarantulas	
Cost Type	**Cost Estimate**
Purchase Price	$15 to $40 (£13.50 to £36)
Tank	$10 to $20 (£9 to £18)
Substrate	$10 (£9)
Decorations	$25 to $50 (£22.50 to £45)
Lighting/Heating	$15 to $35 (£13.50 to £18)
Accessories	$25 to $50 (£22.50 to £45)
Total	$100 to $205 (£90 to £185)

Chapter Two: What to Know Before You Buy

Monthly Costs

After you've covered the initial costs to set up your tarantula cage and to buy your new pet you then need to think about the costs associated with up-keeping the tank. The main recurring cost you need to think about is food for your tarantula. You also need to consider the cost of new substrate, utility costs, and veterinary costs. You will find an overview of these costs below:

Substrate – You will need to perform daily spot treatments of your tarantula cage which means that you might have to add a little bit of new substrate to the tank on a daily basis. Additionally, you will need to completely replace all the substrate in your tank every two to three months when you perform a complete cleaning. As was mentioned in the last section, a large bag of substrate will cost about $10. If you go through one bag every two to three months, your average monthly cost is about $5 (£4.5).

Utilities – In order to keep your tarantula cage at the proper temperature you'll need to keep your heat mat running at all times. This shouldn't have a significant impact on your utilities but you should budget for about $5 (£4.5) monthly.

Chapter Two: What to Know Before You Buy

Veterinary Care – Tarantulas do not require regular veterinary check-ups like traditional pets do. There may, however, come a time when your tarantula gets sick and you need to seek treatment. Most veterinarians are not trained to care for tarantulas so you will need to take your spider to an exotics vet. Not only can it be difficult to find a vet trained to handle tarantulas, but the cost of the visit could be fairly high, between $75 and $100 (£68 to £90). If you take your tarantula to the vet once per year, the average monthly cost is about $7 (£6).

Additional Costs – In addition to the cost of substrate, utilities, and veterinary care you might also have to cover unexpected costs on occasion. These costs might include new cleaning supplies, replacements for tank decorations, or repairs to your tarantula tank. Additional costs may vary and you won't necessarily have to worry about them every month, but you should budget for about $10 (£9) a month just to be prepared.

Monthly Costs for Rose Hair Tarantulas	
Cost Type	Cost Estimate
Substrate	$5 (£4.5)

Chapter Two: What to Know Before You Buy

Utilities	$5 (£4.5)
Veterinary Care	$7 (£6)
Additional Costs	$10 (£9)
Total	$27 (£24)

Chapter Two: What to Know Before You Buy

5.) Pros and Cons for Rose Hair Tarantulas

Before you make your final decision regarding whether or not the rose hair tarantula is the right species for you, take the time to think about the pros and cons for this species. It is important to familiarize yourself with the benefits as well as the drawbacks of this in order to make your choice. Below you will find a list of pros and cons for the rose hair tarantula:

Pros for the Rose Hair Tarantula

- Generally a very docile species, unlikely to attack or bite a human unless threatened
- Very attractive and unique-looking species
- Moderately large species, can be kept in a 10-gallon tank or terrarium
- Typically a low-maintenance species, can adapt to different temperatures and habitats
- Generally a healthy species, not affected by many diseases
- Typically a very quiet pet – does not make any noise
- Doesn't need to be fed everyday – it will be okay if you have to go out of town

Chapter Two: What to Know Before You Buy

Cons for the Rose Hair Tarantula

- Some people find tarantulas intimidating because they are large spiders
- Rose hair tarantula bite can be painful, but it is not medically significant
- Requires you to raise or purchase live insects as food
- Not the kind of pet that enjoys handling
- Males of the species are relatively short-lived compared to females (5 years vs. 20 years)

Chapter Three: Purchasing Rose Hair Tarantulas

By now you should have learned enough about the rose hair tarantula to determine whether or not it is the right pet for you. If it is, your next step is to learn where to purchase one of these animals. In this chapter you will receive some basic information about finding rose hair tarantulas for purchase and for selecting a reputable breeder or supplier. You will also receive tips for choosing a healthy rose hair tarantula – this is important because if you bring home a tarantula that is unhealthy from the start, it is unlikely to thrive and may end up dying soon after you buy it.

Chapter Three: Purchasing Rose Hair Tarantulas

1.) *Where to Buy Rose Hair Tarantulas*

When it comes to purchasing rose hair tarantulas, it may not be as simple as walking into your local pet store. The rose hair tarantula is by far one of the most popular species kept as a pet, however. This means that if your local pet store *does* stock tarantulas, there is a good chance that it will be a rose hair tarantula. If you can't find a tarantula at your local pet store, your next best bet is to go online and search for a breeder. If you cannot find any local breeders online, don't be afraid to ask around at local pet stores or attend a local exotic pet show for ideas.

2.) Selecting a Supplier or Breeder

There are a number of important factors to consider when shopping for a tarantula supplier or breeder. The most important thing to check for is a valid breeding license. Although the United States and the United Kingdom do not require a license to keep tarantulas as pets, breeders are required to obtain a permit. When shopping for a breeder, check the website or ask the breeder directly whether he is licensed and ask for the license number so you can check for verification.

Chapter Three: Purchasing Rose Hair Tarantulas

Once you've determined that the breeder in question is properly licensed you can move on to other considerations. Do not be afraid to call up the breeder and ask questions – it is well worth your time to make sure you buy from a reputable breeder. If you buy your tarantula from an inexperienced hobby breeder you run the risk of buying a tarantula that is in poor health. When you speak to the breeder, make sure you ask about his experience with breeding tarantulas in general as well as his experience with rose hair tarantulas in particular.

In addition to determining the breeder's level of experience with rose hair tarantulas, you also want to ask about his breeding practices. Rose hair tarantulas are fairly easy to breed in captivity, but there is a certain process you should follow. Female rose hair tarantulas should be subjected to a cooling period for several months before the male is introduced. The female should then be kept in good condition for the next few weeks as her egg sac develops.

Chapter Three: Purchasing Rose Hair Tarantulas

3.) Picking a Healthy Tarantula

Before you actually pick out your rose hair tarantula, you need to learn enough about the species to be able to identify it. An inexperienced breeder might try to sell you a different species of tarantula, so know what to look for. You should also be familiar enough with normal tarantula anatomy and behavior to make sure that the spider you are buying is in good health and free from injuries.

<u>Below you will find a collection of things to look for in a healthy rose hair tarantula:</u>

- The color should be fairly uniform across the entire body – there may be patches where urticating hairs have been ejected.
- The spider should possess eight legs, each with seven segments – make sure the legs are all whole.
- Check to make sure the tarantula's pedipalps are also present and uninjured.
- Observe the tarantula in motion to make sure that it doesn't appear to be moving strangely.
- Check the body of the tarantula to make sure it isn't carrying any bugs or parasites.
- Make sure the tarantula isn't preparing to molt – it may be lying on its back with its legs in the air – it is unwise to disturb a tarantula in molt.

Chapter Three: Purchasing Rose Hair Tarantulas

- If the tarantula is standing above the water dish, make sure it is actually drinking – if the spider is hovering over the dish but not drinking it could be because it is dehydrated from low humidity levels.
- Avoid purchasing any tarantula that stands with its legs curled under the body – this usually means that the tarantula is nearing death.
- Ask whether the tarantula is male or female and inquire about its age – males usually only live about 5 years while females can live to be 20.
- Make sure that the tarantulas are captive-bred and not wild-caught.

Chapter Four: Preparing Your Tarantula Cage

In order to keep your rose hair tarantula in good health you need to provide it with a habitat that meets its needs. You cannot just throw your tarantula into a glass tank and expect it to thrive – you must cultivate and maintain certain conditions in regard to heat, humidity, lighting, and more. In this chapter you will learn about the basic habitat requirements for rose hair tarantulas and you will receive specific tips for setting up the ideal tank environment.

Chapter Four: Preparing Your Tarantula Cage

1.) Basic Habitat Requirements

When it comes to setting up a habitat for your rose hair tarantula you have several factors to consider including size, safety, heating, humidity, and security. You will find an overview of each of these factors below:

Size – Rose hair tarantulas grow to about 5 inches in length, so you need to provide a tank that is at least two to three times that length. Tarantulas do not need giant cages because they are mostly blind and will feel insecure if their habitat is too exposed. The best size for a rose hair tarantula tank is 5 or 10 gallons. Glass tanks are better than plastic because they conserve heat and humidity more efficiently.

Safety – In addition to the size of your tarantula tank, you also need to think about safety. You want to place your tarantula tank in a quiet location where he will not be disturbed by people or other pets. Avoid using sharp decorations in your tank because they could pose a safety hazard for your spider and use only soft substrates like potting soil or peat moss. You want your tarantula to be able to create a burrow where he can hide when he wants to feel more secure.

Chapter Four: Preparing Your Tarantula Cage

Heating – While lighting is not a significant concern for pet tarantulas, heating is. Most tarantulas are at least partially nocturnal so they tend to prefer dim and gentle lighting – in most cases, ambient light is the best option. In terms of heating, however, you want to keep your rose hair tarantula cage at a stable temperature around 80°F (27°C), give or take a few degrees. To accomplish this you may need to use a heat mat under the substrate in your tank – low-wattage heat lamps can also be used during the winter when additional heating is needed.

Humidity – In addition to keeping your tarantula tank at a certain temperature, you also need to maintain proper humidity levels. Keeping a water dish in the cage may help to maintain humidity but you should also mist the tank with warm water every few days. Ideally, you should aim for a humidity of at least 70% in your spider tank. Choosing the right substrate will help you to maintain humidity levels in your tank as well.

Security – They may not look like it, but tarantulas are notorious escape artists. In order to keep your tarantula tank secure you need to use a tight-fitting lid and you might also want to consider keeping something heavy on top of

Chapter Four: Preparing Your Tarantula Cage

the lid just in case. If possible, a locking lid is even better. Just remember that you need a lid that will allow some air to flow into and out of the tank.

Chapter Four: Preparing Your Tarantula Cage

2.) Setting Up the Cage

Now that you know the basics about habitat requirements for your rose hair tarantula you can think about actually setting up your habitat. Again, you want to start off by choosing a tank that will provide your spider with enough space to move around comfortably. Tarantulas tend not to travel great distances in search of food, however, so the tank doesn't need to be overly large – a 5 to 10 gallon glass tank will be sufficient.

Once you've chosen your tarantula tank then you need to fill it with substrate and decorations. The type of substrate you choose for your tarantula tank is very important

Chapter Four: Preparing Your Tarantula Cage

because your spider will dig into it to create a burrow. You need to make sure to choose a substrate that is completely organic – this simply means that it doesn't contain any inorganic contaminants. The substrate should be soft enough that your spider can burrow into it and it should also help to preserve humidity. Some of the best options include orchid bark, sandy soil, potting soil, vermiculite, and peat moss.

When adding the substrate to your tarantula tank you should make sure that it is at least 3 inches deep so your spider can burrow into it. If you are concerned with the appearance of your tarantula tank, consider lining the bottom of the tank with a 3-inch layer of sandy soil or potting soil then add a layer of orchid bark or peat moss on top of it. Your substrate should be kept damp, but not wet – you can accomplish this by misting the tank every few days. Test the dampness of the substrate by pinching it – it should be just damp enough to clump but shouldn't drip.

After lining the bottom of your tank with substrate you then need to think about what kind of tank furnishings you want to use. To give your spider a place to start his burrow you should include a small piece of cork bark or driftwood – a small half-log will be fine as well. You can include additional decorations like sticks, rocks, and live or fake plants in your tank as well. Just make sure that any heavy

Chapter Four: Preparing Your Tarantula Cage

decorations you use are nestled into the substrate for support in case your spider climbs on them.

Chapter Four: Preparing Your Tarantula Cage

3.) Lighting and Heating Requirements

After you have set up and decorate your rose hair tarantula tank you then need to think about lighting and heating requirements. As you have already learned, most tarantulas prefer dim or gentle lighting – they may be stressed out by bright lighting so stick to ambient light if you can. You want to avoid using overhead lighting not just because it will stress your spider, but because it can also cause water in the tank to evaporate which could have a negative impact on the humidity in your tank.

Although lighting is not a major concern for tarantula cages, heating is very important. The rose hair tarantula comes from a naturally warm and humid environment so you want to mimic those conditions in your tank. The best temperature for a rose hair tarantula is about 80°F (27°C) but you have a little bit of wiggle room in either direction. To maintain the proper temperature in your tank you'll need to install a heat mat under the bottom of the tank – this will keep the substrate in your tank warm. If you live in a very cold climate you might also have to use heat lamps to maintain the right temperature, but make sure they are low-wattage.

Keeping your tarantula tank warm will also help to keep the humidity level up. The ideal humidity level inside your

Chapter Four: Preparing Your Tarantula Cage

rose hair tarantula's burrow is 70% so you should aim for a total tank humidity somewhere between 60% and 80%. Having a dish of water in your tank will help to keep the humidity up but you may also need to mist your tank with a spray bottle of warm water every few days. Make sure the substrate in your tank stays damp, but not wet – this is the best way to maintain humidity.

Chapter Four: Preparing Your Tarantula Cage

4.) Cage Cleaning and Maintenance

Once you have set up your tarantula tank, all that is left is to maintain it. Your main task for tank maintenance will be to maintain proper heat and humidity levels. You should also think about various cleaning tasks as well, however. Keep an eye out for decaying organic matter in the tank and remove it promptly so it doesn't attract mites or cause fungus and mold to grow in the tank. The main culprit will usually be uneaten food, so be sure to remove any uneaten food the day after feeding.

When your tarantula is molting you need to be extra careful about tank maintenance. Clean up the remains of

Chapter Four: Preparing Your Tarantula Cage

your tarantula's shed exoskeleton as quickly as possible. You also need to be very mindful of removing uneaten prey items immediately because your tarantula will be vulnerable while his new exoskeleton is growing in. Keep an eye on your spider during feeding and remove uneaten insects as soon as possible.

Each day you should do a spot-cleaning of the tank to remove soiled substrate and to refresh the water in your water dish. In addition to this daily spot cleaning you should also perform a thorough tank cleaning every two to three months. Remove the substrate and decorations from the tank and wipe it down with a mild soap-and-water solution. Scrub your tank decorations clean and rinse well then add new substrate to the tank and place your decorations back in the tank. The only time you should skip this major tank cleaning is if your spider is molting.

Chapter Five: Feeding Your Tarantula

One of the most important things you can do to keep your tarantula healthy is to provide it with a healthy diet. The diet of tarantulas is very different from that of more traditional pets like cats and dogs, so you need to take the time to learn about your tarantula's nutritional needs and what you can do to meet them. In this chapter you will find an overview of the nutritional needs for tarantulas as well as the different types of food your tarantula is likely to eat. You will also receive some basic feeding tips for the rose hair tarantula.

Chapter Five: Feeding Your Tarantula

1.) Basic Nutritional Needs

Feeding a tarantula is a little bit different from feeding a traditional pet like a cat or dog. If you have a cat you can just go to the pet store and pick up a bag of cat food. For a rose hair tarantula, things are not quite so simple. Before you bring home your new pet you need to learn about its basic nutritional needs so you can provide a healthy diet. The main thing you need to know about the rose hair tarantula's nutritional needs is that these spiders are primarily insectivorous – this means that insects comprise the majority of their diet.

Rose hair tarantulas will eat a wide variety of different insects and some will even eat the occasional pinky mouse (baby mouse). This being the case, the diet of the rose hair tarantula might more accurately be described as carnivorous. Tarantulas do not need to be fed every day. In most cases, your tarantula will only eat once or twice per week. If your spider is molting, he may not even eat at all. On the other side of the spectrum, tarantulas sometimes gorge themselves and then fast for a period of several weeks up to a month.

In addition to choosing the right prey items for your rose hair tarantula, you also need to make sure you are preparing his prey properly. Rose hair tarantulas do not eat

Chapter Five: Feeding Your Tarantula

plant matter so the only nutrients they receive are those provided by insects. To make sure that your tarantula gets the vitamins and minerals that insects lack you should be gut-loading your insects. This simply means that you should feed your prey insects a healthy diet of fruits and vegetables so that when your tarantula eats the insects, it also consumes the nutritious foods the prey ate.

2.) Types of Tarantula Food

Rose hair tarantulas will eat a wide variety of insects, depending what is available. Crickets are by far the most popular type of tarantula food and most tarantulas will eat three to five large crickets on a weekly basis. You can also offer your tarantula other feeder insects of similar size. This includes mealworms, wax worms, small roaches, small locusts, grasshoppers, beetles and more. These insects should always be offered live so they will be the most appealing to your tarantula. You should also feed your tarantula at night when he is most likely to be active.

Chapter Five: Feeding Your Tarantula

3.) Feeding Tips for Tarantulas

The frequency with which your rose hair tarantula eats may vary but you should aim to offer him food about twice per week. Make sure you space out your feedings with several days in between and only offer live prey. Your tarantula may not eat the food as soon as you offer it, so you can leave it in the tank for up to 24 hours. Remove any uneaten insects from the tank at this point so they do not cause a problem. If your spider is molting, remove uneaten insects immediately after feeding because your spider will be vulnerable as his new exoskeleton grows in until it becomes fully hardened.

You might be tempted to save money on food for your tarantula by catching wild insects for food. Unfortunately, wild-caught insects have the potential to carry disease which could be passed on to your tarantula. You should always purchase your feeder insects from a pet store or supplier. If you really want to save money, consider raising insects yourself.

Chapter Six: Breeding Rose Hair Tarantulas

Breeding rose hair tarantulas has been successfully accomplished in captivity and it is surprisingly easy to achieve. Before you try to breed your own tarantula, however, you should take the time to learn about the tarantula breeding process. In this chapter you will learn the basics about breeding tarantulas including information about sexual dimorphism for the species and tips for preparing your tarantula for breeding. You will also receive tips for raising your spiderlings.

Chapter Six: Breeding Rose Hair Tarantulas

1.) *Basic Breeding Information*

Before you attempt to breed your rose hair tarantula you should learn the basics about tarantula breeding. To start, you should learn how to tell the difference between a male and female rose hair tarantula so you can select a breeding pair. Male rose hair tarantulas are typically a little larger than females with longer legs and fuzzier bodies. The coloring on male tarantulas may also be a little bit brighter. This kind of sexual dimorphism is different than the kind exhibited by many other tarantula species. In other species, the males tend to be smaller and less brightly colored than the females.

Another thing to look for in differentiating between male and female tarantulas is hooks on the front legs. Male tarantulas have tibial hooks on their front legs which they use to restrain the female's fangs during the breeding process. This may be the reason why a male tarantula's legs are longer than a female's. During breeding, the male will hold onto the female and push her into a near vertical position to gain access to her external genitalia.

Because male rose hair tarantulas tend to live much shorter lives than females you need to be intentional about when you choose to breed your tarantula. You also need to keep in mind the fact that most males die within a few

Chapter Six: Breeding Rose Hair Tarantulas

weeks of mating. You will know that your male tarantula is ready for breeding when he spins a sperm web. This type of web is usually woven on a flat surface and the male creates it by rubbing his abdomen on the surface while releasing his semen. He then inserts his pedipalps into the semen and absorbs some of it in preparation for breeding.

Chapter Six: Breeding Rose Hair Tarantulas

2.) Tips for Breeding Your Tarantula

If you plan to breed your rose hair tarantula you should start conditioning your female several months before you want the actual breeding to occur. Female rose hair tarantulas benefit from a cooling period during which the temperature in the cage is slightly reduced. Once the male spins his semen web you can then introduce the male tarantula into the female's cage. The male will quickly detect the presence of the female and he will begin tapping his legs on the ground, signaling to the female and lulling her into a receptive state.

Chapter Six: Breeding Rose Hair Tarantulas

Once the female tarantula is receptive to mating, the male will approach her burrow and wait for the opportune moment. At this time, the male will lunge forward and grab the female, using the hooks on his front legs to retract her fangs. The male will push the female into a near vertical position so he can gain access to her external genitalia, the epigyne. The male will then dip his pedipalps into the epigyne, using either one or both, to inject his semen.

After a successful mating, the male tarantula will flee the scene quickly. Female tarantulas often exhibit aggression following mating, but they generally do not attack or eat the male. Still, the male tarantula is unlikely to live more than a few weeks after breeding. After fertilization, the female will develop a very large egg sac in which she deposits anywhere between 50 and 2,000 eggs (the average for the rose hair tarantula is about 500). Over the next 6 to 8 weeks, the female will guard the egg sac, turning it often to keep the eggs from becoming deformed.

Once the spiderlings hatch from their eggs, they remain inside the next for several days, feeding off the remains of their yolk sac before they disperse. The first spiders to leave the nest are called nymphs – they look like spiders but they are all white in color and they will be very small. At this point you should remove the female from the tank and raise the nymphs separately. The nymphs will be unlikely to feed

Chapter Six: Breeding Rose Hair Tarantulas

until they have molted once or twice, at which point they can be considered spiderlings.

In order to make sure that your spiderlings can find their prey, you should keep them in a fairly small container – baby food jars are a good option as long as you drill tiny holes in the lid for ventilation. Your containers should be filled about halfway with soft substrate like garden soil or vermiculite. Use a pencil or something similar to make a depression in the center of the container – this will act as a starter burrow for the spiderlings. You do not need to add water to the container until the spiderlings grow larger – they will get the water they need from their prey.

The best food for spiderlings is small crickets and other insects. As a general rule, you should be offering your spiderlings insects that are about the length of the spiderling's body. Pinhead crickets and baby cockroaches are a good option, as are termites and maggots. Do not use fruit flies because they are too small and their ability to fly will make them hard for the spiderlings to catch. Try to feed your spiderlings about twice a week and remove any dead or uneaten food the next day.

Chapter Seven: Keeping Your Tarantula Healthy

Keeping your rose hair tarantula in good health can be a challenge since there are so many different factors to consider. Not only do you have to provide your tarantula with the proper environment, but you also have to feed it the right diet. Even if you do these things, however, your tarantula could still fall ill. In this chapter you will find an overview of common conditions affecting the rose hair tarantula so you can be prepared to deal with them, should they arise.

Chapter Seven: Keeping Your Tarantula Healthy

1.) Common Health Problems

In general, tarantulas are not prone to many diseases. In most cases, if your tarantula gets sick it is probably due to contamination through wild-caught insects, tank decorations that haven't been thoroughly cleaned, or contaminated substrate. To make sure your rose hair tarantula remains in good health you should familiarize yourself with the conditions to which this species might be prone so you can identify them and quickly start your spider on the right course of treatment.

Conditions affecting tarantulas may include:

- Bad molt
- Dehydration
- Fungal infection
- Mites
- Nematode worms
- Trauma

Chapter Seven: Keeping Your Tarantula Healthy

Bad Molt

While your rose hair tarantula is molting he will be very vulnerable. Tarantulas do not have bones – they have a hard exoskeleton on the outside of their bodies. While they are molting, they actually shed that exoskeleton and the new one grows in underneath but the new exoskeleton will be soft at first. This being the case, your tarantula will be extra vulnerable to injury and even the insects you feed it could be dangerous.

In addition to making your tarantula more vulnerable, molting can sometimes go wrong. If your tarantula is not properly hydrated his body could dry out which could cause problems with molting. Molting problems, or bad molt, most commonly affects very young spiders, very old spiders, and spiders that are malnourished. Premature molting can also cause a problem if the carapace splits before it should.

The best way to make sure that your tarantula's molt goes according to plan is to be very careful. Make sure to remove insects from the cage immediately after feeding if your spider doesn't eat them. You should also monitor the humidity level in your tarantula cage to make sure your spider is properly hydrated for a molt.

Chapter Seven: Keeping Your Tarantula Healthy

Dehydration

For tarantulas, dehydration can be very serious – especially species like the rose hair tarantula that come from a naturally warm and humid climate. In many cases, spiders do not drink water so the only moisture they get is from the prey they consume. Just because your spider doesn't drink water, however, doesn't mean that he doesn't need it. Keeping your humidity level in your tarantula cage high is another good way to keep your spider from becoming dehydrated.

If you see your spider standing over the water bowl but he isn't actually drinking, it could mean that he is dehydrated and is trying to hydrate himself. Other signs of dehydrate in spiders include lethargy, wrinkled body, and a shriveled or shrunken appearance. Providing your spider with a bowl of fresh water may help – just be sure that the water level is low enough that if your spider enters the bowl he won't drown. You should also mist your tarantula cage to make sure the humidity level is high enough.

Chapter Seven: Keeping Your Tarantula Healthy

Fungal Infection

When it comes to keeping your tarantula cage at the right humidity level it is a fine line to walk. If the humidity in your tank is too low, your tarantula will become dehydrated. If the humidity is too high, however, it could promote the growth of mold and fungus. Mold can be very dangerous for tarantulas because it often causes fatal internal organ infections.

When the infection first sets in it will appear as a cream-colored spot on the abdomen, carapace, or legs. If you do not treat the infection immediately it could spread quickly and your tarantula could die. The best treatment is to immediately transfer your spider to a clean and well-ventilated cage. You can also try applying betadine to the infected area as treatment.

By the time you notice a fungal infection in your tarantula, it will probably already be too late. This is why prevention is the best option. Do your best to maintain a stable humidity level in your tarantula tank around 70% and avoid misting the tank too frequently. If your tarantula does get a fungal infection, immersing him in a 10% alcohol solution might help as a last-ditch effort to keep the spider from dying.

Chapter Seven: Keeping Your Tarantula Healthy

Mites

One of the most common issues affecting the rose hair tarantula is mites. Mites appear as tiny reddish-brown spots that generally affect the areas around the eyes and mouth, though they can also appear on your spider's body or in the tank substrate. In many cases, you might not even be able to see the mites but you can see their effects on your spider – his health will decline slowly but surely.

Unfortunately, there are no topical treatments for mites in spiders like there are for mites in cats and dogs. Mites are particularly likely to become a problem in tanks where the humidity level is not stable. You cannot treat your spider with anything to kill the mites but you can remove them manually. Just put a little bit of petroleum jelly on the end of a cotton swab and touch it to the mites on your spider's body. The mites will stick to the petroleum jelly and you can then discard the swab.

Chapter Seven: Keeping Your Tarantula Healthy

Nematode Worms

Nematode worms are a type of internal parasite infection and it can be extremely serious for your tarantula. Once your tarantula comes down with an internal parasite infection he will no longer be able to eat and his health will decline rapidly. You may not notice any symptoms at first other than not eating, but eventually the spider may start to display unusual behaviors. These behaviors could include restlessness, spinning a lot of silk, refusal to leave the water dish, or a gummy white mass forming at the mouth. You may also notice a sickly sweet odor in your tank.

Unfortunately, there is no effective treatment for nematode worms in tarantulas. There is a treatment in development by the Research Institute for Exotic Species Microbiology, but nothing has become available yet. Your best bet is to prevent nematode infections by keeping your tarantula tank clean and within the proper humidity level. You should also take care to avoid contamination with dirty substrate or tank decorations and avoid feeding your tarantula wild-caught insects.

Chapter Seven: Keeping Your Tarantula Healthy

Trauma

Rose hair tarantulas are generally not affected by many diseases, but they are prone to certain types of trauma. Injuries are very common among tarantulas because they can hurt themselves falling from tank decorations or when trying to scale the tank walls. Your spider could also be injured if a tank decoration falls over on top of him. In some cases, tarantula owners have also injured their spiders with rough handling.

In many cases, even injuries that seem minor can become very dangerous if left untreated. Spiders do not bleed in the traditional sense, but they do lose hemolymph (the whitish substance that serves the same function as blood). Your best bet to treat open wounds is to close them with super glue. If your spider loses a let he may be able to grow it back during his next molt, but the loss of hemolymph could be fatal – he might also have trouble molting properly after the loss of the limb. For all of these reasons, you need to take precautions against injury for your tarantula.

Chapter Seven: Keeping Your Tarantula Healthy

2.) Tips for Preventing Disease

There are two main things you should do in order to reduce your tarantula's risk for getting sick. First, you always need to keep your tarantula tank clean. Perform daily spot cleanings to remove soiled substrate and to refresh the water bowl. Perform a larger total-tank cleaning every two or three months and replace the substrate completely. Additionally, you should avoid feeding your spider wild-caught insects because they are likely to be carriers of disease.

In addition to knowing the basics about maintaining your tarantula cage and preventing disease, you should also

Chapter Seven: Keeping Your Tarantula Healthy

brush up on tarantula first-aid. Tarantulas are prone to very few illnesses - which is good news for you as a tarantula owner - but they are prone to injury. If your tarantula falls from a great height or if one of your tank decorations falls on him, he could become injured. The best first-aid tool to have on hand for tarantulas is super glue.

If your tarantula sustains a bleeding injury, super glue is your best bet. As you've already learned, tarantulas do not have "true blood" but they do have a similar substance called hemolymph that serves the same role. If your tarantula injures himself you'll need to stop the flow of hemolymph and mend the wound – super glue is the easiest and most effective way to do that. If your tarantula happens to lose a limb you can use super glue to close the wound and the spider will grow a new leg during his next molting period.

Chapter Eight: Frequently Asked Questions

By now you should have a thorough understanding of the rose hair tarantula and how to care for it. Even if you have read through this entire book, however, you might still have questions. In this chapter you will find a collection of some of the most frequently asked questions about the pet tarantula as well as the rose hair tarantula in particular. The answers to these questions will help you to learn more about this species so you can become the best tarantula owner you can be.

Chapter Eight: Frequently Asked Questions

Q: *Why do rose hair tarantulas make good pets?*

A: Rose hair tarantulas are a very popular species because they are so docile and easy to maintain. This species is not one of the largest species of tarantula so you can keep it in a moderately sized tank, and they generally do not bite or attack humans unless they feel threatened. Even if the rose hair tarantula does bit, it is likely to only cause pain – it is not a medical emergency.

Q: *Is it better to buy a male or a female tarantula?*

A: The answer to this question is largely a matter of preference. Male rose hair tarantulas are larger and more colorful than females, but they have a much shorter lifespan (especially if you breed them). In terms of temperament, there are no discernible differences between the sexes.

Q: *Do rose hair tarantulas bite? Is it dangerous?*

A: The rose hair tarantula does possess venom, but it is designed to take down small prey like insects – it is unlikely to cause a serious reaction in humans. The bite of a rose hair tarantula is about as painful as a bee sting, though it may throb or ache for a little while. Be sure to clean the wound properly to prevent infection.

Chapter Eight: Frequently Asked Questions

Q: *Can I buy a rose hair tarantula online?*

A: Although the rose hair tarantula is one of the most commonly kept species of pet tarantula, you may not be able to find one just by walking into your local pet store. Buying tarantulas online allows you to shop for an experienced breeder and to compare prices. Just be sure that the person you buy from carries the proper license.

Q: *Are there any laws related to tarantulas I should know?*

A: The laws affecting tarantula owners and breeders vary from one area to another. In both the United States and the United Kingdom, a permit or license is not required to keep a rose hair tarantula. There are always exceptions to the rule however (for example, it is illegal to keep tarantulas in New York City), so be sure to check with your local council to be safe. There are laws regarding the import/export of tarantulas as well as breeding. You may also need to be careful about animal welfare laws, particularly in the U.K. In the U.K. it is illegal to feed live animals to one another (like feeding live mice to snakes), but this particular rule generally doesn't apply to the rose hair tarantula because it only eats insects.

Chapter Eight: Frequently Asked Questions

Q: *What exactly is molting?*

A: Molting is the process through which a tarantula grows a new exoskeleton to replace the old one – it is similar to shedding in snakes and other reptiles. While the rose hair tarantula is young it may molt several times a year as it grows. Once the tarantula reaches maturity, however, it will usually only molt once per year. Some tarantulas will molt more often if they need to replace a limb or a section of urticating hairs that has been lost.

Q: *What should I do if my tarantula bites me?*

A: If you suffer a Chilean rose tarantula bite, you do not need to panic. The bite might be painful, but it is unlikely to cause any systemic reaction. All you have to do is clean the wound and treat it with a topical antiseptic to prevent a secondary infection.

Q: *Why do I need to wear safety glasses when handling my rose hair tarantula?*

A: For the most part, the rose hair tarantula is not a dangerous or aggressive species. Like any animal, however, the tarantula will defend itself if it feels threatened. One of the main defense mechanisms this tarantula has is the

Chapter Eight: Frequently Asked Questions

urticating hairs on its abdomen. These hairs are covered in tiny barbs which can become embedded in your skin or eyes if the tarantula feels threatened and chooses to eject them at you.

Q: *What is the proper way to handle my tarantula?*

A: Even though rose hair tarantulas are a docile species, you still need to handle them with care. The safest way to pick up your tarantula is to grip it between the second and third pair of legs – you can also place your hand on the ground and nudge the spider into it. Once you've picked up the tarantula, keep it in the palm of your hand and be very careful not to let it fall.

Chapter Nine: Rose Hair Tarantula Care Sheet

By the time you finish this book you should have a firm understanding of what the rose hair tarantula is and how to care for it. Once you bring your tarantula home, you can then refer back to this book for information when you need it. You may find, however, that you need to reference certain facts but you do not want to skim through the entire book to find them – that is where this care sheet comes in. In this chapter you will find a rose hair tarantula care sheet that summarizes all of the most important tarantula facts and information in one easy-to-use reference guide.

Chapter Nine: Rose Hair Tarantula Care Sheet

1.) Basic Information

Scientific Name: *Grammastola rosea*

Taxonomy: family Theraphosidae

Country of Origin: Chile

Distribution: northern Chile, Argentina, and Bolivia

Habitat: desert and scrub regions

Size: average 5-inch (12.5cm) leg span

Maturity: reach adult size between 3 and 4 years

Color: dark brown to black with a coat of reddish or pink hairs on the body

Anatomy: two-part body covered in an exoskeleton; eight legs, each with seven segments

Molting: shedding the exoskeleton in order to grow; young tarantulas might molt several times a year, mature tarantulas once a year or less

Temperament: docile and low-maintenance

Lifespan (male): average 15 to 20 years

Lifespan (female): average 4 to 5 years

Chapter Nine: Rose Hair Tarantula Care Sheet

Diet: primarily insects including crickets, locusts, grasshoppers, cockroaches, mealworms, etc.

Breeding: breed fairly easily in captivity; females produce egg sacs containing about 500 eggs

Sexual Dimorphism: males have longer legs and a fuzzier appearance; females are stocky and bulky

Chapter Nine: Rose Hair Tarantula Care Sheet

2.) Habitat Set-Up Information

Habitat Needs: space, safety, heating, humidity, security

Tank Size: 5 to 10 gallons

Tank Materials: glass is preferable to plastic

Safety: keep the tank in a quiet location away from people and pets; avoid sharp decorations; use soft substrates

Lighting: not a significant concern; ambient lighting is best

Heating: maintain stable temperature around 80°F (27°C); use heat mat and low-wattage heat lamps

Humidity: aim for at least 70%; keep water dish in tank and mist it every few days

Security: use a tight-fitting lid, ideally a locking lid; make sure lid allows for air exchange

Substrate: should be soft and moist; best options include orchid bark, sandy soil, potting soil, vermiculite, peat moss

Furnishings: cork bark, driftwood or half-log for burrow; sticks, rocks and live or fake plants

Cage Maintenance: daily spot cleaning; thorough cleaning and substrate replacement every 2 to 3 months

3.) Feeding Information

Diet Type: primarily insectivorous; may also be carnivorous

Feeding Frequency: offer food twice weekly; some will eat more or less often and may gorge themselves before fasting for several weeks

Preparing Prey: gut-load feeder insects with nutritious foods like fruits and vegetables

Feeder Insects: crickets, mealworms, wax worms, small roaches, small locusts, grasshoppers, beetles

Feeding Instructions: offer only live prey; insects should be gut-loaded prior to feeding

Feeding Time: offer food at night when the tarantula will be most active

Feeding Cautions: do not feed wild-caught insects because they could carry disease

4.) Breeding Information

Sexual Dimorphism (male): longer legs, brighter color, tibial hooks on front legs

Sexual Dimorphism (female): slightly smaller, slightly dull coloration

Ready for Breeding (male): spins a sperm web, dips pedipalps to collect semen

Ready for Breeding (female): several months cooling period prior to breeding

Breeding Behavior: introduce male to female; male taps legs to signal female

Mating Process: male lunges at females, restrains her fangs with tibial hooks; dips pedipalps into epigyne to fertilize

After Mating: male retreats quickly; female may become aggressive

Fertilization: female forms an egg sac and deposits eggs

Number of Eggs: 50 to 2,000 (average 500)

Egg Development: eggs develop over 6 to 8 weeks

Hatching: eggs hatch in the nest, young remain inside until they absorb the remains of their yolk sac

Chapter Nine: Rose Hair Tarantula Care Sheet

Spiderlings: emerge from the nest as nymphs, become spiderlings after two molts

Feeding Young: twice per week; small crickets and other insects; size of the spiderlings' bodies

Housing Young: small containers (ex: baby food jars with tiny holes drilled in lids)

Chapter Ten: Relevant Websites

In reading this book you have received a wealth of information about the rose hair tarantula including facts about tarantulas, tarantula care, feeding tarantulas and more. When you bring your own tarantula home, you will be able to use this book as a guide. Even though this book is filled with useful information, you may still find that you have questions or that you need help finding supplies for your new pet. In this chapter you will find a collection of relevant websites and useful resources regarding cages, cage accessories, and food for tarantulas.

Chapter Ten: Relevant Websites

1.) Cages for Rose Hair Tarantulas

In this section you will find a collection of useful resources and websites for cages for rose hair tarantulas.

United States Websites:

Glass Aquariums. Fish Tanks Direct.
<http://www.fishtanksdirect.com/Glass_Aquariums.aspx>

Fish Tanks and Aquariums. PetSmart.
<http://www.petsmart.com/fish/aquariums/cat-36-catid-300065>

Glass Aquariums and Tanks. Marineland.
<http://www.marineland.com/Products/glass-aquariums-and-tanks.aspx>

Tarantula Cages. TarantulaCages.com.
<http://www.tarantulacages.com/>

How to Set Up Your Tarantula Cage. TarantulaPets.com.
<http://www.tarantulapets.com/tarantula-cages/>

Chapter Ten: Relevant Websites

United Kingdom Websites:

All Glass Aquariums. JunglePets.
<http://www.junglepets.co.uk/all-glass-aquariums-36-c.asp>

High-Quality Aquarium Glass. AquariumGlass.co.uk.
<http://www.aquariumglass.co.uk/>

Terrariums and Enclosures. The Spider Shop.
<http://www.thespidershop.co.uk/terrariums-tanks-c-36_62.html>

Glass Tanks. Amazon.co.uk.
<http://www.amazon.co.uk/aquariums-fishtanks/b?ie=UTF8&node=471501031>

Standard Terrestrial Tarantula Setup.
<http://terrestrialtarantulas.blogspot.co.uk/2011/01/chaco-golden-knee-caresheet-grammostola.html>

Chapter Ten: Relevant Websites

2.) Cage Accessories and Decorations

In this section you will find a collection of useful websites and resources for cage accessories and decorations for rose hair tarantulas.

United States Websites:

Sphagnum Peat Moss. The Home Depot.
<http://www.homedepot.com/p/Miracle-Gro-Sphagnum-Peat-Moss-85278430/204502292>

Reptile Food & Water Accessories. PetSmart.
<http://www.petsmart.com/reptile/food-water-accessories/cat-36-catid-500005>

Repti-Therm Under Tank Heater. ZooMed.
<http://zoomed.com/db/products/EntryDetail.php?EntryID=113&DatabaseID=2&SearchID=5>

How to Make a Pet Tarantula Tank You Can Be Proud Of.
<http://www.petful.com/other-pets/how-make-pet-tarantula-habitat/>

Chapter Ten: Relevant Websites

United Kingdom Websites:

Bulk Irish Peat Moss. Evergreen.
<http://www.evergreenpeat.co.uk/IMP_Bulk.php>

Driftwood Decorations. Amazon.co.uk.
<http://www.amazon.co.uk/s/ref=nb_sb_ss_c_0_9?url=search-alias%3Dpets&field-keywords=driftwood&sprefix=driftwood%2Coutdoor%2C247>

Aquarium Plants Live. Seapets.
<http://www.seapets.co.uk/products/aquarium-supplies/aquarium-plants-live/>

Zoo Med Repti-Therm Heat Mat. Online Reptile Shop.
<http://www.onlinereptileshop.co.uk/reptile-products/Specialist-Heating/Zoo-Med-Repti-therm-Heat-Mat-8x18inch-Rh6-eu-4555.html#sthash.zsLuXSnA.dpbs>

The Never-Ending Substrate Debate. Tarantula's Burrow.
<http://arachnophiliac.info/burrow/substrate.htm>

Chapter Ten: Relevant Websites

3.) Food for Rose Hair Tarantulas

In this section you will find a collection of resources and suppliers for food for rose hair tarantulas.

United States Websites:

Live Crickets. Fluker Farms.
<http://www.flukerfarms.com/crickets.aspx>

Mealworms. Petco.com.
<http://www.petco.com/product/12678/Mealworms.aspx

Rainbow Mealworms and Crickets.
<http://www.rainbowmealworms.net/>

Live Crickets, Worms and Supplies. Drs. Foster & Smith.
<http://www.drsfostersmith.com/reptile-supplies/reptile-foods/live-crickets-worms-feeding-supplies/ps/c/6016/7891/8900

Food and Diet. Tarantula Guide.
<http://www.tarantulaguide.com/tarantulas-food-water-diet/>

Chapter Ten: Relevant Websites

United Kingdom Websites:

Mealworms – Live and Dried. LiveFoodsDirect.
<http://www.livefoodsdirect.co.uk/Category/Mealworms>

Komodo Feeder Insects Enhancing Formula. 888Reptiles.
<http://www.888reptiles.co.uk/3800.html>

Feeder Insects. Reptile Realm.
<http://reptilerealm.co.uk/category/feederinsects/>

Black Crickets. LiveFoodsDirect.
<http://www.livefoodsdirect.co.uk/Category/Black-Crickets>

All About Tarantula Feeding. Pets4Homes.
<http://www.pets4homes.co.uk/pet-advice/all-about-tarantula-feeding.html>

Chapter Ten: Relevant Websites

4.) Additional Resources and Supplies

In this section you will find a collection of additional resources and references for rose hair tarantulas.

United States Websites:

Beginner's Guide to Tarantula Care. Tarantula-Care.com.
<http://tarantula-care.com/beginners-guide-to-tarantula-care/>

Keeping Tarantulas as Pets. Pet-Spider.
<http://www.pet-spider.com/>

Chilean Rose Hair Tarantula. Tarantula Guide.
<http://www.tarantulaguide.com/tarantulas/chilean-rose-hair-tarantula/>

Basic Tarantula Care. TarantulaCages.com.
<http://www.tarantulacages.com/tarantulacare.html>

Tarantulas as Pets. LLL Reptile.
<http://www.lllreptile.com/articles/106-tarantulas-as-pets

Chapter Ten: Relevant Websites

United Kingdom Websites:

Basic Tarantula Care Sheet. The Tarantula's Burrow.
<http://arachnophiliac.info/burrow/caresheets/basic_care.htm>

Tarantula Care Sheet. TC Reptiles.
<http://www.tcreptiles.co.uk/tarantulacare.htm>

Chilean Rose Tarantula Care Sheet. The Reptilian.
<http://www.thereptilian.co.uk/care_sheets/chilean_rose_tarantula_grammostola_rosea_care_sheet.html>

New World Tarantula Spider. Animal Corner.
<https://animalcorner.co.uk/animals/new-world-tarantula-spider/>

Keeping Tarantulas – The Basics. The BTS.
<http://www.thebts.co.uk/keeping_tarantulas.html>

Chile Rose Tarantula. Exotic-Pets.co.uk.
<http://www.exotic-pets.co.uk/chile-rose-tarantula.html.

Index

A

abdomen	9, 10, 11, 12, 14, 17, 25, 28, 72, 80, 90
aggressive	27, 89, 96
ambient light	56, 61
animal	10, 11, 39, 88, 89, 120
appearance	13, 16, 20, 30, 32, 59, 79, 93
Arachnida	9
arachnids	9

B

beginner	27
behaviors	82
bite	7, 17, 25, 46, 47, 87, 89
blood	10, 83, 85
body	9, 10, 11, 14, 16, 19, 24, 28, 30, 52, 53, 75, 78, 79, 81, 92
breeder	36, 40, 48, 49, 50, 51, 52, 88
breeding	17, 29, 35, 50, 51, 70, 71, 72, 73, 74, 88, 96
budget	42, 43, 44
burrow	26, 55, 59, 62, 74, 75, 94, 102, 106, 120

C

cage	31, 40, 43, 56, 73, 78, 79, 80, 84, 98, 101, 119
captivity	17, 18, 20, 31, 51, 70, 93
care	8, 17, 34, 40, 44, 82, 86, 90, 91, 98, 105, 106, 119, 121
care sheet	91
carnivorous	66, 95

cephalothorax	10, 11, 14
Chile	16, 19, 22, 92, 106
cleaning	42, 43, 44, 63, 64, 84, 94
cockroaches	17, 20, 75, 93
color	16, 21, 22, 52, 74, 96
coloration	26, 30, 32, 96
conditions	28, 54, 61, 76, 77
contamination	77, 82
cost	34, 40, 41, 42, 43, 44, 120
Costa Rican Zebra	23, 26, 27
crickets	17, 20, 27, 68, 75, 93, 95, 97, 103
Curly Hair Tarantula	23, 30

D

dangerous	14, 35, 78, 80, 83, 87, 89
decorations	41, 44, 55, 58, 59, 64, 77, 82, 83, 85, 94, 101
defense	12, 17, 89
Dehydration	77, 79
Desert Blonde	23, 28
diseases	46, 77, 83
docile	3, 7, 17, 19, 25, 32, 46, 87, 90, 92
drawbacks	46
driftwood	41, 59, 94, 102

E

eating	18, 82
egg sac	18, 51, 74, 96
eggs	18, 20, 74, 93, 96
endoskeleton	14
environment	54, 61, 76
escape	27, 56
exoskeleton	10, 11, 14, 18, 19, 64, 69, 78, 89, 92

eyes	17, 81, 90

F

facts	13, 91, 98
fangs	9, 10, 71, 74, 96, 114
feeding	31, 63, 64, 65, 66, 69, 74, 78, 82, 84, 88, 95, 98, 103, 104
females	11, 16, 20, 24, 29, 31, 33, 47, 53, 71, 87, 93, 96
food	11, 43, 47, 58, 63, 65, 66, 68, 69, 75, 95, 97, 98, 101, 103
fungus	63, 80
furnish	40

G

genitalia	10, 71, 74
glands	11
grasshoppers	17, 20, 27, 68, 93, 95
gut-loading	67

H

habitat	8, 25, 33, 54, 55, 58, 101, 119
hair	3, 7, 8, 11, 13, 14, 16, 17, 18, 21, 22, 23, 27, 30, 31, 34, 35, 36, 37, 39, 40, 41, 46, 47, 48, 49, 51, 52, 54, 55, 56, 58, 61, 62, 65, 66, 68, 69, 70, 71, 73, 74, 76, 77, 78, 79, 81, 83, 86, 87, 88, 89, 90, 91, 98, 99, 101, 103, 105, 114, 115, 119, 120, 121
healthy	8, 46, 48, 52, 65, 66, 67, 121
heat lamp	42
heat mat	17, 41, 43, 56, 61, 94
history	13
humidity	17, 27, 31, 42, 53, 54, 55, 56, 59, 61, 63, 78, 79, 80, 81, 82, 94
hunt	21, 27

I

infection	77, 80, 82, 87, 89
information	3, 8, 13, 34, 48, 70, 91, 98
initial costs	40, 43
injury	78, 83, 85
insectivorous	39, 66, 95
insects	17, 20, 27, 29, 31, 47, 64, 66, 67, 68, 69, 75, 77, 78, 82, 84, 87, 88, 93, 95, 97
internal	10, 80, 82
invertebrates	10, 39, 121

L

laws	88
leg	7, 10, 11, 12, 15, 17, 19, 24, 26, 27, 85, 92
leg span	7, 15, 17, 19, 24, 27, 92
legal	35
license	35, 50, 88
licensing	34
lifespan	18, 31, 87
lighting	17, 41, 54, 56, 61, 94
limb	9, 83, 85, 89
lizards	29
locusts	17, 20, 68, 93, 95

M

males	11, 20, 24, 29, 33, 53, 71, 93
maturity	17, 24, 33, 89
mealworms	17, 20, 68, 93, 95
Mexican Fireleg	23, 32, 33
Mexican Redknee	23, 24, 32
mice	31, 88

Rose Hair Tarantula   P a g e | 113

minerals	67
mites	9, 63, 81
mold	63, 80
molt	18, 19, 52, 77, 78, 83, 89, 92
molting	18, 63, 64, 66, 69, 78, 83, 85, 89

N

Nematode	77, 82
night	11, 21, 68, 95
nocturnal	17, 21, 28, 56
nutritional needs	65, 66
nymphs	74, 97

O

opithosoma	9
orchid bark	59, 94
organs	9, 11

P

parasite	82
peat moss	55, 59, 94
pedicel	14
pedipalps	52, 72, 74, 96
pet	3, 8, 13, 14, 16, 17, 22, 23, 31, 33, 34, 37, 39, 40, 43, 46, 47, 48, 49, 56, 66, 69, 86, 88, 98, 101, 104, 105, 119, 120, 121
pet show	49
pet store	40, 49, 66, 69, 88
prevention	80
prey	12, 39, 64, 66, 69, 75, 79, 87, 95
pros and cons	34, 46
prosoma	9, 14

protein	10, 11
purchase	35, 40, 41, 42, 47, 48, 69

Q

questions	37, 51, 86, 98
quiet	46, 55, 94

R

requirements	34, 35, 54, 58, 61
research	17
resources	98, 99, 101, 103, 105

S

safety	55, 89, 94
scientific name	21
segment	10, 11
semen	72, 73, 74, 96
sexual dimorphism	70, 71
sexual maturity	33
shed	10, 11, 18, 64, 78
silk	11, 82
size	14, 19, 32, 41, 55, 68, 92, 97
skin	17, 90
skittish	17, 27
soil	55, 59, 75, 94
species	3, 7, 8, 9, 11, 14, 16, 17, 18, 21, 22, 23, 24, 25, 26, 27, 28, 30, 31, 32, 34, 35, 37, 38, 39, 46, 47, 49, 52, 70, 71, 77, 79, 86, 87, 88, 89, 90
sperm	72, 96
spider	7, 9, 10, 11, 12, 13, 18, 21, 28, 44, 52, 53, 55, 56, 58, 59, 61, 64, 66, 69, 77, 78, 79, 80, 81, 82, 83, 84, 85, 90, 105, 106, 114
spiderlings	70, 74, 75, 97, 120

spinning	11, 82
substrate	27, 41, 43, 44, 56, 58, 59, 61, 62, 64, 75, 77, 81, 82, 84, 94, 102
super glue	83, 85
supplies	44, 98, 102, 103

T

tank	40, 41, 42, 43, 44, 46, 54, 55, 56, 58, 59, 61, 63, 64, 69, 74, 77, 80, 81, 82, 83, 84, 85, 87, 94
tarantula	3, 7, 8, 9, 13, 14, 15, 16, 17, 18, 21, 22, 23, 24, 26, 27, 28, 30, 31, 32, 34, 35, 37, 38, 39, 40, 41, 42, 43, 44, 46, 47, 48, 49, 50, 51, 52, 53, 54, 55, 56, 58, 59, 61, 63, 65, 66, 68, 69, 70, 71, 73, 74, 76, 77, 78, 79, 80, 81, 82, 83, 84, 85, 86, 87, 88, 89, 90, 91, 95, 98, 99, 101, 104, 105, 106, 114, 117, 118, 119, 120, 121
temperature	17, 31, 43, 56, 61, 73, 94
terrarium	17, 38, 46
thermometer	42
Trauma	77, 83
types	13, 65, 83

U

urticating hairs	17, 25, 52, 89, 90
utility	43

V

vermiculite	59, 75, 94
vet	44
vitamins	67

W

water	28, 42, 53, 56, 61, 62, 64, 75, 79, 82, 84, 94, 101, 103
web	21, 72, 73, 96
wild-caught	35, 53, 69, 77, 82, 84, 95

Photo Credits

Cover Page Photo By Pixabay User PaigeH, <https://pixabay.com/en/tarantula-spider-fuzzy-fangs-797095/>

Page 1 Photo By Viki via Wikimedia Commons, <https://en.wikipedia.org/wiki/Chilean_rose_tarantula#/media/File:Grammostola_cf._porteri_adult_male.jpg>

Page 13 Photo By Factumquintus via Wikimedia Commons, <https://zh.wikipedia.org/wiki/%E6%99%BA%E5%88%A9%E7%B4%85%E7%8E%AB%E7%91%B0%E8%9C%98%E8%9B%9B#/media/File:Grammostola_rosea_adult_weiblich.jpg>

Page 16 Photo By Moe Epsilon via Wikimedia Commons, <https://commons.wikimedia.org/wiki/File:Rose_hair_tarantula_(Grammostola_rosea)_at_Petco_in_Jacksonville,_Florida.jpg>

Page 24 Photo By George Chernilevsky via Wikimedia Commons, <https://en.wikipedia.org/wiki/Mexican_

redknee_tarantula#/media/File:Brachypelma_smithi_2009_G09.jpg>

Page 26 Photo By Termininja via Wikimedia Commons, <https://en.wikipedia.org/wiki/Aphonopelma_seemanni#/media/File:Aphonopelma_seemanni_front_view.jpg>

Page 28 Photo By Snake Collector via Wikimedia Commons, <https://en.wikipedia.org/wiki/Aphonopelma_chalcodes#/media/File:Aphonopelma_chalcodes.jpg>

Page 30 Photo By Sarefo via Wikimedia Commons, <https://en.wikipedia.org/wiki/Brachypelma_albopilosum#/media/File:Brachypelma.albopilosum.female.jpg>

Page 32 Photo By Ltshears via Wikimedia Commons, <https://en.wikipedia.org/wiki/Brachypelma_boehmei#/media/File:Tarantula_Image_002.jpg>

Page 34 Photo By Yastay via Wikimedia Commons, <https://commons.wikimedia.org/wiki/File:Grammostola_rosea_03.JPG>

Page 37 Photo By Ltshears via Wikimedia Commons, <https://commons.wikimedia.org/wiki/File:Chilean_Rose_Hair_2.jpg>

Page 48 Photo By Fae via Wikimedia Commons, <https://commons.wikimedia.org/wiki/File:Rose_Hair_Tarantula_(19197476340).jpg>

Page 50 Photo By Psychonaught via Wikimedia Commons, <https://commons.wikimedia.org/wiki/File:Grammostola_rosea_Chilian_Rose_Hair_Tarantula.jpg>

Page 54 Photo By Flickr user Cliff1066, <https://www.flickr.com/photos/nostri-imago/2892872168/sizes/o/>

Page 58 Photo By Flickr user Spencer77, <https://www.flickr.com/photos/spencer77/4890868356/sizes/l>

Page 63 Photo By Flickr user Janoma.cl, <https://www.flickr.com/photos/janoma/4166601791/sizes/l>

Page 65 Photo By Flickr user Balthazira, <https://www.flickr.com/photos/47529564@N04/4558861262/sizes/l>

Page 68 Photo By Flickr user Fixed in Silver, <https://www.flickr.com/photos/daniellesimone/9472587143/sizes/l>

Page 70 Photo By Dawson via Wikimedia Commons, <https://commons.wikimedia.org/wiki/File:Mating_rose_hair_tarantulas.jpg>

Page 73 Photo By Flamesbane via Wikimedia Commons, <https://en.wikipedia.org/wiki/Cobalt_blue_tarantula#/media/File:2iH_lividum.JPG

Page 76 Photo By Rollopack via Wikimedia Commons, <https://commons.wikimedia.org/wiki/File:Grammostola_rosea_young.jpg>

Page 84 Photo By Sarefo via Wikimedia Commons, <https://en.wikipedia.org/wiki/Urticating_hair#/media/File:Grammostola.rosea.with.hair.patch.jpg>

Page 86 Photo By Domser via Wikimedia Commons, <https://de.wikipedia.org/wiki/Datei:Grammostola_cf._porteri_-_adult_female.jpg

Page 91 Photo By Flickr user Cliff1066, <https://www.flickr.com/photos/nostri-imago/3017358632/sizes/o/>

Page 98 Photo By Ltshears via Wikimedia Commons, <https://commons.wikimedia.org/wiki/File:Chilean_Rose_Hair_Tarantula_2.jpg>

References

"Ailments and Treatments for Tarantulas." Animals.mom.me. <http://animals.mom.me/ailments-treatments-tarantulas-1283.html>

"Aphonopelma chalcodes." Animal Diversity Web. <http://animaldiversity.org/accounts/Aphonopelma_chalcodes/>

"Basic Tarantula Care." Tarantulas.com. <http://www.tarantulas.com/care_info.html>

"Beginner's Guide to Tarantula Care." Tarantula-Care.com. <http://tarantula-care.com/beginners-guide-to-tarantula-care/>

"Cage and Habitat." Tarantula Guide. <http://www.tarantulaguide.com/pet-tarantula-cage-and-habitat/>

"Chilean Rose Hair Tarantula." Pet Supplies Plus. <http://www.petsuppliesplus.com/content.jsp?pageName=rose_hair_tarantula>

"Choosing a Tarantula." Tarantulas.com. <http://www.tarantulas.com/choosing.html>

"Costa-Rican Zebra Tarantula." The Tarantula's Burrow. <http://arachnophiliac.info/burrow/caresheets/aphonopelma_semmanni.htm>

"Glossary of Spider Terminology." Spiders.us. <http://www.spiders.us/glossary/>

"Handling." Tarantula Guide. <http://www.tarantulaguide.com/handling-pet-tarantulas/>

"How Much Does a Tarantula Cost?" Howmuchisit.org. <http://www.howmuchisit.org/how-much-does-a-tarantula-cost/>

"How to Know if a Pet Tarantula is Sick." eHow.com. <http://www.ehow.com/how_2049525_know-pet-tarantula-ill.html>

"Raising Young Tarantulas." Tarantulas.com. <http://www.tarantulas.com/spiderlings.html>

"Rose Hair Tarantula." LLL Reptile. <http://www.lllreptile.com/articles/38-rose-hair-tarantula>

"Rose-Haired Tarantula." Animal-World Encyclopedia. <http://animal-world.com/encyclo/reptiles/spiders/rosehairtarantula.php>

"Rose Hair Tarantula Care Sheet." Exotic Pets Resources. <http://www.exoticpetsresources.com/invertebrates/rose-hair-tarantula/rose-hair-tarantula-care-sheet/>

"Tarantula First Aid." Tarantulas.com. <http://www.tarantulas.com/first_aid.html>

"Tarantula Importing and Arachnid Commerce." Exotic Fauna. <http://exoticfauna.com/arachnoculture/2/AC-i2a5-p1.html>

"Tarantula Reproduction." Tarantulas Fauna World. <http://tarantulas.tropica.ru/en/node/571>

"Tips for Choosing and Buying a Healthy Pet Tarantula." Pets4Homes. <http://www.pets4homes.co.uk/pet-advice/tips-for-choosing-and-buying-a-healthy-pet-tarantula.html>